© 2021 Sunbird Books, an imprint of Phoenix International Publications, Inc.

| 8501 West Higgins Road | 34 Seymour Street | Heimhuder Straße 81 |
| Chicago, Illinois 60631 | London W1H 7JE | 20148 Hamburg |

This library edition published 2024.

www.sunbirdkidsbooks.com

Library of Congress Control Number: 2023932432

ISBN: 979-8-7654-0305-1 Printed in China

V Is for VOTES!

A SUFFRAGETTE ALPHABET

Written by Erin Rose Wage   Illustrated by Jane Pica

sunbird books

A is for amendment.

The 19th Amendment to the United States Constitution allowed women to vote.

August 26, 1920
the 19th
Amendment
was added to
the Constitution.

B is for bloomers.

Skirts used to be *so heavy* that women had to lift them to move. Light bloomers let women walk more comfortably—toward the ballot box!

C is for Carrie Chapman Catt.

Carrie Chapman Catt was a leader of the suffrage movement.

D is for Declaration of Sentiments.

The Declaration of Sentiments was written by a group of women who wanted freedom.

...He has never permitted her to exercise her inalienable Right to the elective franchise...

E is for equal.

The Declaration of Independence states: "all men are created equal." The Declaration of Sentiments added two words: "all men **and women** are created equal."

F is for Seneca Falls.

Seneca Falls, New York, is where the first women's rights meeting was held. There, the Declaration of Sentiments was read.

G is for Matilda Joslyn Gage.

Activist Matilda Joslyn Gage wrote a book about the history of the suffrage movement.

H is for Harriet Tubman.

Harriet Tubman was a suffragist who gave powerful speeches about her experience as an enslaved woman.

I is for Ida B. Wells.

Journalist Ida B. Wells founded one of the first Black American suffrage groups.

J is for justice.

Justice means treating everyone fairly. When women fought for their right to vote, they fought for justice!

K is for Florence Kelley.

Florence Kelley was a suffrage leader who fought for child labor laws to keep children safe.

L is for Lucretia Mott.

When Lucretia Mott was not allowed in anti-slavery meetings because she was a woman, she planned the first women's rights convention.

M is for Mary Church Terrell.

Mary Church Terrell was a suffrage activist who earned several college degrees—at a time when very few women were allowed to.

N is for Nina Allender.

Artist Nina Allender drew pictures about the fight for the vote. Her cartoons made people laugh, cry, and *think*.

VOTES FOR WOMEN!

O is for organize.

Organize means to gather people to work on something together. Suffrage activists organized marches and protests for women's rights.

P is for Alice Paul, PhD.

Alice Paul made a flag and sewed a star on it for each state that agreed to the 19th Amendment.

P is *also* for purple!

Purple, gold, and white are the colors of the suffrage movement.

Q is for Quaker.

Many Quakers fought for women's suffrage because Quakers believe that all people are equal.

LUCRETIA MOTT

ALICE PAUL

SUSAN B. ANTHONY

R is for Hattie Redmond.

Hattie Redmond organized meetings in her home state of Oregon, which granted female suffrage in 1912!

VOTES FOR WOMEN

S is for suffrage.

Suffrage means having the right to vote in elections. Suffragists and suffragettes fight for voting rights for *all* citizens.

T is for Sojourner Truth.

Sojourner Truth traveled the country speaking truth about the wrongness of slavery and the rightness of equality.

U is for United States v. Susan B. Anthony.

Susan B. Anthony was arrested for voting in 1872. Although she was found guilty, her trial brought positive attention to the suffragists' cause.

V is for votes.

A vote is a mark of a citizen's choice on a ballot during an election.

W is for
Dr. Mary Edwards Walker.

Dr. Mary Edwards Walker was arrested for dressing in "men's clothes." She fought for suffrage and for a woman's right to choose her own clothing.

X marks her vote!

Y is for you!

You have the right to vote when you are 18 years old! Right now, how can you continue the work of your foremothers to help the women of the world speak out against injustice?

Z is for Zitkála-Šá.

Zitkála-Šá, of the Yankton Dakota Sioux, was a writer, musician, and activist who fought for Native American suffrage.